Contents

Introducing Pakistan

Just over fifty years ago, in 1947, a new country was born: Pakistan, which means 'Land of the Pure'. Lying between Afghanistan and India, Pakistan is a land of many different landscapes and peoples. It is made up of five main provinces, and controls part of Jammu and Kashmir, which is disputed territory that lies between Pakistan and India. The capital city, Islamabad, is home to the Shah Faisal Mosque, which is visited and worshipped at by millions of people each year.

▲ Crowds of shoppers at Empress Market, in Karachi. This bustling, crowded city was once the capital of Pakistan. It is still a major industrial and trading centre and has a busy sea port.

◀ Donkeys are still used in many villages for carrying loads.

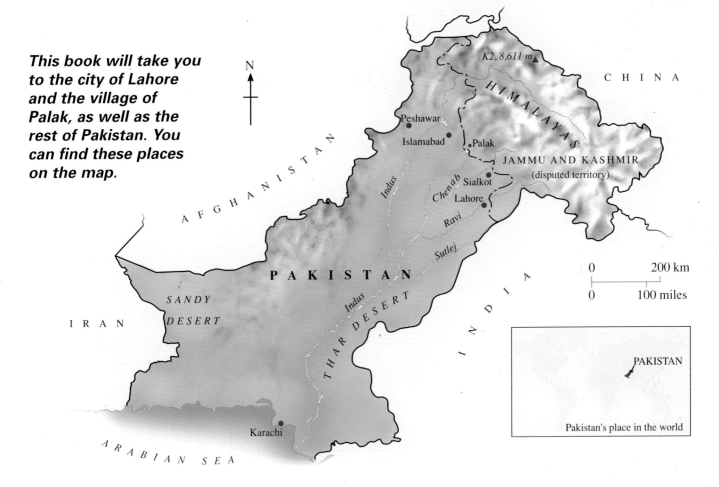

This book will take you to the city of Lahore and the village of Palak, as well as the rest of Pakistan. You can find these places on the map.

Over 4,500 years ago, the area that is now Pakistan was home to the ancient Indus Valley civilization. There were well-planned cities, with ancient public baths, and people wrote using a complicated system of writing. Since then, the land has been ruled by many different peoples.

When Pakistan was first formed, in 1947, the country was made up of two parts, East and West Pakistan. In 1971, East Pakistan became the separate country of Bangladesh and the west side became the Pakistan we know today. Since then, there have been many improvements in farming and industry, which have provided lots of new jobs and made the country more wealthy.

PAKISTAN FACTS	
Population:	131.4 million
Total land area:	796,100 km²
Currency:	Pakistani rupee
Religions	
Muslim:	97%
Other:	3%

Sources: *World Bank Atlas 1995;*
Pakistan Tradition and Change (Oxfam, 1996)

The city of Lahore

Lahore, often called 'the heart of Pakistan', is the second-largest city in Pakistan. The Persians, Afghans, Mughals, Sikhs and British have all ruled Lahore in the past, and each culture has left its influence on the style of the city's buildings.

Today, Lahore has an old city centre, with newer industrial areas and housing to the south. The old city has quite overcrowded living conditions, but it is a good place to go shopping in the evenings when the bazaars open. The most expensive shops, selling exclusive clothes and perfumes, are found in the Gulberg area and the Fortress Stadium.

LAHORE

Population: 2.953 million

Source: 1981 Census

▼ *Lahore Fort, with the city in the background. The old Mughal city of Lahore, which contains elegant buildings and beautiful gardens, was originally surrounded by high, strong walls with twelve huge gates.*

Since Lahore is the capital of the Punjab province, it contains official buildings, such as the High Court and Government House, as well as modern office blocks and banks. It is also a city of many parks, including Bagh-i-Jinnah, where the largest flower show in Pakistan is held. There is a museum, known locally as *Ajaib Ghar* (meaning 'Wonder House'), famous universities and colleges, a cathedral and a zoo. The Minar-e-Pakistan is a tower in Lahore that commemorates the signing of the Declaration of Independence in 1940, which led to the creation of Pakistan, seven years later.

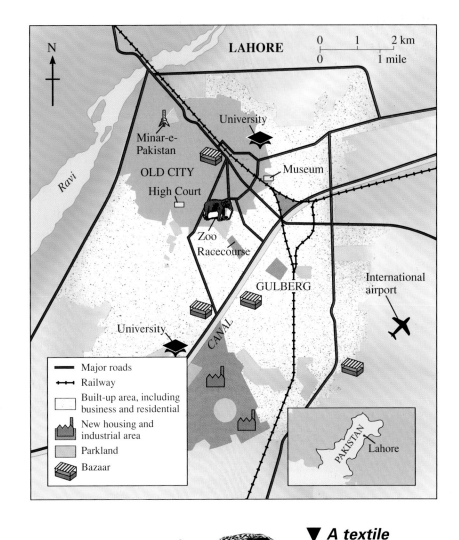

LAHORE

Major roads
Railway
Built-up area, including business and residential
New housing and industrial area
Parkland
Bazaar

▼ *A textile trader in one of Lahore's bazaars.*

The village of Palak

Palak is a village of about 200 homes in the north-east of Pakistan. It lies in a region called Jammu and Kashmir, which is controlled partly by Pakistan, and partly by India. Palak is in the part controlled by Pakistan. A trip from Palak to Lahore takes about four hours by bus.

Since 1967, when the Mangla Dam was built, Palak has been on the shore of a huge reservoir. The Mangla reservoir stores water for irrigating farmland and generating electricity. When the dam was first built, over 100,000 people had to move away from the land that was flooded.

▲ *Palak village with the Mangla reservoir in the distance. The reservoir has a shoreline of 400 km and covers an area of over 240 km².*

'Everybody knows everyone else in the village. We try to help each other, especially older people – it is part of our religion and culture.' – Gulzar Hussain, villager.

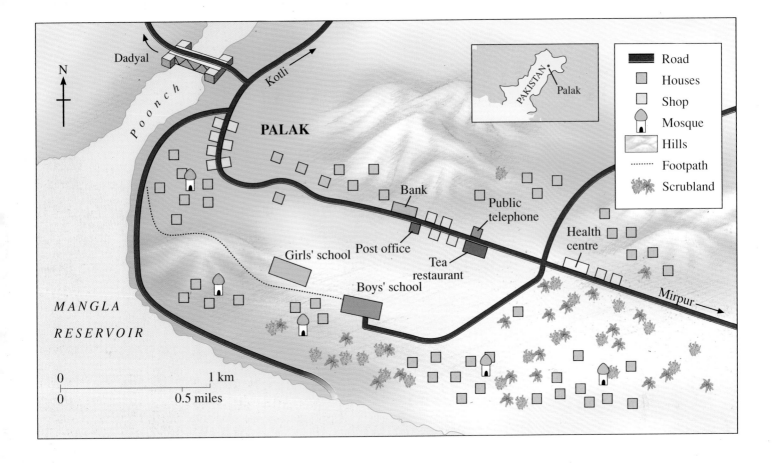

Many people have left Palak to live in other parts of Pakistan, or moved abroad. Their relatives in the village now enjoy quite a good standard of living because they are sent money from countries such as Britain, Saudi Arabia, the USA and the Netherlands.

The majority of people living in Palak are involved in farming wheat and other crops on the fertile, silty soils of the area. The village has good shops and services, including a bank, post office, fruit shops, a butcher's, a barber and one medical centre with five health workers.

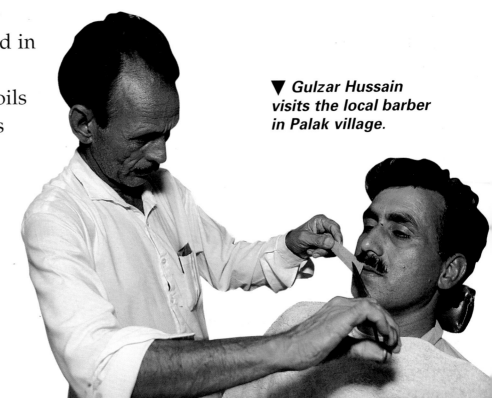

▼ *Gulzar Hussain visits the local barber in Palak village.*

Land and climate

Pakistan has many different types of landscape. In the mountainous north is the world's second-highest mountain, called K2, where glaciers flow down the sides of snowy peaks. Southern Pakistan has some of the world's hottest deserts and on the coast there are tropical beaches. The River Indus begins its life in the northern mountains and flows the length of the country, growing in size as it is joined by four other major rivers. These rivers water the fertile flood plains of the Punjab province, where most of Pakistan's population live. Where the River Indus meets the Arabian Sea, there is a huge delta of mangrove swamps and lagoons.

▼ *A man walks around a rock face above the River Indus, in the far north of Pakistan. The beautiful scenery of the mountainous north attracts many visitors each year.*

PAKISTAN'S CLIMATE			
	Average annual rainfall	Average daily temperature	
		January	August
Karachi	125 mm	17.5 °C	30 °C
Lahore	500 mm	10 °C	31 °C
Palak	1,000 mm	5 °C	25 °C

Source: *Atlas of Pakistan* (Survey of Pakistan & Rawalpindi, 1990)

The climate in Pakistan varies according to the landscape. Parts of the mountainous north have a climate like the Arctic, and temperatures can fall to –20 °C. Much of the central and southern areas of the country have a desert-type climate, and temperatures can soar to 50 °C. Most of the country has a mild winter, lasting from November to March, and a summer from April to September. Heavy rains usually fall in July and August each year, and there are often floods in some areas. Earthquakes are common in the mountainous north and west of Pakistan.

▲ *Camels outside a village on the edge of the Thar Desert, in the far south-east of Pakistan. Camels are an ideal form of transport in this type of landscape.*

◄ *A farmer uses oxen to plough a field on a fertile hillside in the Punjab province.*

11

City on a flood plain

Lahore lies on the flood plains of the River Ravi, one of the five great rivers of the Punjab province. The city is surrounded by farmland, which is irrigated by water channels from the river. Crops such as wheat, barley, maize and chickpeas are grown, as well as vegetables, such as potatoes and turnips, and fruit such as oranges and melons.

Summers in Lahore are dry and hot. When given the choice, most people prefer to stay indoors out of the sun during the day and come out in the evening.

▼ *A boy washes his feet using a water pump above a tube well. Water is not far below the ground here.*

▲ *Cattle grazing on the banks of the Ravi river in Lahore. The bridge connects the city with Ravi Town, on the western side of the river.*

The hot weather means that working days generally start and finish earlier in summer than in winter. When the monsoon begins, in July, the air becomes very humid. Winter days can be quite warm, but it is very cold at night. Sometimes it can be quite foggy in the mornings and evenings, and occasionally there is a frost.

Much of the farmland around Lahore suffers from waterlogging, where water does not drain away from the soil. Rainwater dissolves minerals in the soil and becomes salty. When the water evaporates, salt crusts are left on the surface of the soil. These make it difficult for crops to grow.

▲ *Fishing on a stretch of the Ravi river near Lahore.*

Flooding from the River Ravi used to be a big problem in the land around the city, until an embankment was built alongside the river in 1960. The embankment means the water in the river can be controlled.

Beside a reservoir

The village of Palak lies on the banks of the Mangla reservoir in the Poonch river valley. It is on the edge of a range of high, sandstone hills, called the Pia Punjal range, in the Himalayan foothills. Many of the plants on the hills have spiky leaves, which help the plants to store more water through the hot and dry times of the year.

In the winter there is snow on the mountains, which melts when the temperature starts to rise in April. The melting snow makes the River Poonch flow very fast into the reservoir, which is at its fullest in June and July.

▼ *When the reservoir is full, many village houses lie right next to the water's edge.*

During the summer monsoon season, from July to September, heavy rainstorms can cause major flooding. In September 1992, the floodgates of the Mangla Dam had to be opened to stop water flowing over the top of the dam walls. As a result, many people died when an island downstream was flooded.

Terraced farming and forestry are important around Palak. Crops such as wheat and corn, and plants used for animal food are grown on plots of land separated by thorny bushes. When the reservoir water level is low, fertile, silty soils are uncovered. There is just enough time between high water-levels each year to plant, grow and harvest a high-quality wheat crop.

▲ *Grass being cut to feed a family's buffalo.*

◄ *Examining a cob of corn before harvesting in late September.*

Home life

Family life is very important in Pakistan. Three generations often live together in the same house, so grandparents help to look after the children while parents go to work. Sometimes, where families share a business, two brothers live together with their wives and children. In towns and cities, many more families are now just two parents and their children sharing a small house or flat.

Houses often have more than one floor. Traditional homes, called *havali* houses, are two or three stories high. They have a central courtyard with a garden and fountain, and all the rooms lead off it. The bedrooms are usually downstairs.

A food stall at ▶ *Clifton Beach, Karachi.*

FAVOURITE FOODS

Baked and deep-fried breads: *chapattis, nans, rotis,* and *puris.*

Street snacks: *samosas, kebabs* and *tikkas.*

Curries: *dhal* (lentil curry), meat curries, spicy spinach, cabbage and peas and *pillau* rice.

Desserts: sweet rice and *barfi* (sweetened, dried-milk solids in a variety of flavours).

There are usually two bedrooms, a lounge and a small kitchen. Many homes have flat roofs, which are popular places to sit or sleep on *charpois* (traditional string beds). Neighbours often chat to each other across the roof tops.

Most city homes, and a growing number of village homes, have electricity and running water. Wealthy families have expensive Asian carpets, air conditioning, gardens and even swimming pools. In contrast, some homes, like those of Afghan refugees outside the city of Peshawar, are made of clay, mud-bricks, sheets of fabric, wood and corrugated iron.

The Muslim religion is very important for most people in Pakistan. Families get up to say prayers at sunrise and will pray four more times during the day when they hear the call from the local mosque. In most homes, families share a midday meal together.

▲ *Worshipping at a mosque. An imam (religious leader) can be seen leading the prayers.*

◀ *Carpets are stretched and dried on the city's rooftops.*

Home life in Lahore

Homes in the city centre of Lahore are usually older town houses, but there are also modern flats in the suburbs. There are big differences in the quality of life, depending on the wealth of each family.

Iftikhar Hussain lives with his wife and three children in a four-roomed flat, which is about ten minutes' drive from the city centre. Their weekdays are similar to those of many quite wealthy families in Lahore. Iftikhar gets up for prayers at sunrise every morning. He wakes up the rest of the family and drives the children to school on the way to his office, where he works as an accountant. When Iftikhar and the children come home at about 1.30 pm, the family sits down together for lunch.

'When I come home from school, I have a wash and pray before lunch with the rest of the family.'
– Hina Hussain, 9 years old.

▼ *Family life on the roof of a large city house.*

▲ Girls walk to school in one of the narrow streets of the old city.

After lunch, the children then usually do their homework, have home tuition or go for their Arabic class, while Iftikhar goes back to work. At about 9.30 pm, the children go to bed after a family evening meal.

Mustafa Khan works as a government officer. He and his family have a government flat and car. Their comfortable, eight-roomed home is surrounded by gardens and has extra living space for housekeepers, who help the family with washing, cleaning, shopping and cooking. Like many fairly wealthy families, the Khans have air-conditioning, a fridge-freezer, washing machine, video and hi-fi system.

Muhammad Parvaiz and his six children sell *samosas* and other snacks in the old city. The eight family members live in two rooms above a shop, in a large old building near where they work. They share a bathroom with two other families on the roof of the building, up a long winding staircase. Despite the overcrowded conditions, the family gets on very well with their neighbours.

◄ There are lots of snack stalls with places to sit and eat to choose from in Lahore.

Home life in Palak

Almost all homes in Palak are made of bricks and have flat roofs. Their window shutters are often closed to keep out the hot sunlight. Most homes now have running water, toilets and electricity. The Mirza family live in a bungalow with its own plot of land, where vegetables are grown. Bungalows are popular in Palak and there is lots of space for them. The family home has electric fans to help keep the house cool and a television set which they enjoy watching in the evenings. The children often complain when the electricity does not work. This happens when too many people in the area are using electricity at the same time.

▲ **The Mirza family outside their home. Mr Muhammad Yaseen Mirza is the headteacher at the boys' school in Palak.**

◄ **Mrs Mirza cooking the family dinner.**

Everyone knows each other in Palak and people tend to get on well. If someone comes to the village and needs a place to stay, it is seen as a duty to look after them.

Religion is very important to people in Palak. There are about ten mosques in the village, including one main mosque. On most days, people will go to their local mosque to hear the local imam. On Fridays, people go to the Jamia mosque, where the special prayers '*Salat al-Jum'ah*' are said.

During election time, there is a lot of attention given to politics and who to vote for.

▲ *Shopping at a local store in the village. Most villagers' daily needs can be bought in the shops in Palak.*

'When I was a boy, I used to have to climb up the hills to collect water. Now, we have a tank and pipes to bring water to our homes.'
– Gulzar Hussain, villager.

Pakistan at work

There are many different jobs in Pakistan, from professional jobs such as teaching, medicine and the law, to manual jobs such as farming, industrial work or street trading. Parents often have high expectations for their children, and law and medicine are popular careers young people aim for.

Pakistan's industry includes cotton and clothing, cement, chemicals and fertilizers, sugar refining and heavy engineering. There are steel mills near Karachi, and Pakistan has a Suzuki factory which makes cars and vans from parts shipped in from Japan. The city of Sialkot is world famous for the sports equipment made there, especially hockey sticks and cricket bats. The footballs used in the 1990 World Cup were made in Sialkot.

▼ *One of Pakistan's many chemical factories. The increase in technology and industry in Pakistan means that a wide range of modern goods can now be produced.*

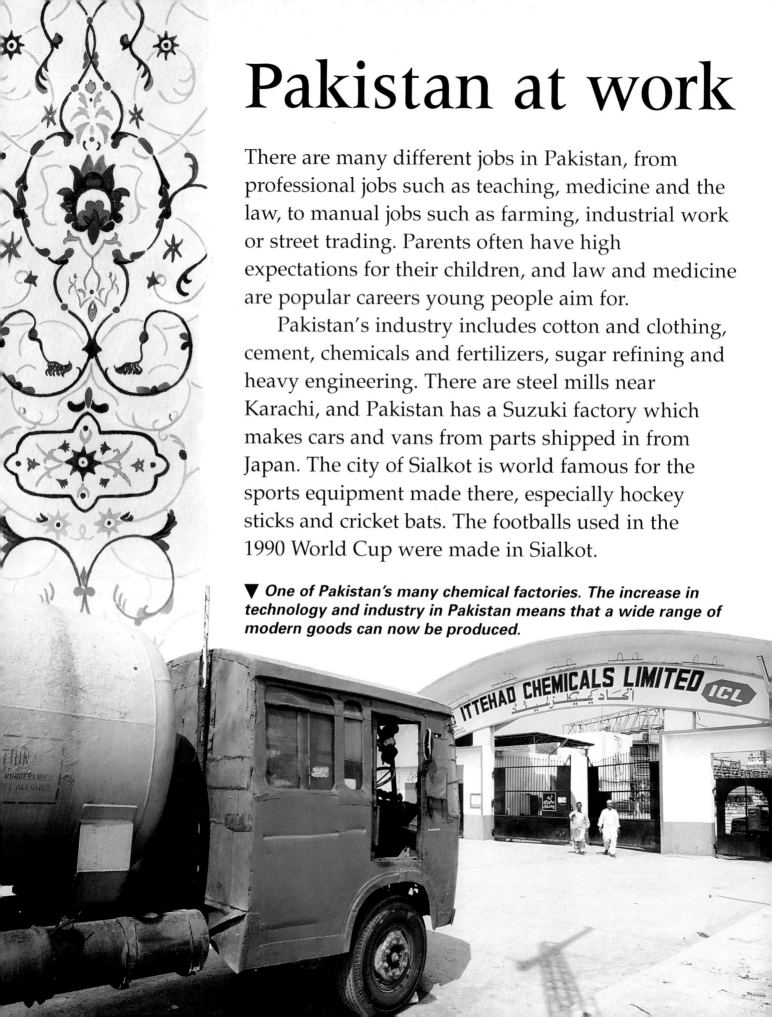

A farmworker carries cut grass to be fed to his family's buffalo. Many farmers in Pakistan use buffalo, which are very strong, to help them plough the fields.

TYPE OF WORK IN PAKISTAN	
	Percentage of population
Agriculture	46%
Manufacturing	18%
Services	17%
Other	19%
	Source: *The World Bank Atlas, 1995*

About half of the working population of Pakistan is involved in farming, which provides most of the income for people in rural areas. The most widely grown crops are wheat, cotton, sugar cane and rice. Life is especially busy at harvest times, in April and October. The government is encouraging more industry in rural areas to help stop so many people moving to the cities.

Skilled craftspeople throughout Pakistan produce goods such as jewellery, silks, embroidery, leatherwork, woodwork, pottery and world-famous carpets.

About 10 per cent of Pakistan's male workers leave the country to work in oil-producing countries of the Middle East, especially Saudi Arabia, where better-paid jobs can be found.

Making furniture by hand in Karachi, which will then be sold abroad. There are still many skilled craftspeople in Pakistan.

23

Work in Lahore

Lahore is a city where people work in a whole variety of jobs. Most work is either in shops, crafts production, working in small businesses, or in the civil service, law courts or universities. There is a great demand for taxi and scooter rickshaw drivers in this busy city. Many drivers borrow money to buy a vehicle which they use to earn their living.

Aftab Raja works in one of Lahore's bazaars as a tailor. He measures customers and can produce finished outfits called *shalwar kameezes* for them within a day.

▲ *Cutting out metal sheets in a small factory in Lahore.*

Children working in ▶ a motorcycle repair shop. Some children leave school early to earn money to help their families.

A few streets away are tiny workshops, where copper and brass are beaten into shape and sold in a bazaar devoted to copper and brass goods. Afghan refugees sell carpets from all over Asia at Shadman Bazaar, while gold jewellery is crafted by goldsmiths in the high-class Mall area of the city.

In the Gulberg area, women work behind the counters of large shops, selling perfume, clothing, toys and household items. Street hawkers all over the city carry and sell items ranging from plastic cups to antiques. The whole city seems to be involved in creating, making and selling.

Larger industries, some set up by foreign companies, lie on the southern edge of the city. They include leather and knitwear factories, and a steel-processing plant.

A laboratory technician ▶ working at the Shaukat Khanum Memorial Cancer Hospital.

Work in Palak

Most people in Palak are involved in growing and harvesting wheat and maize. The Masud family grow wheat on terraced land inherited from Mr Masud's father, and on the silty soil left when the water-level in the reservoir falls after October each year. The deep mud can be dangerous for farmers, but no time can be wasted because wheat seeds need to be planted as soon as possible. The crop is just ready to harvest as the water-level starts to rise again in April or May. The family have to pay people to help them cut the crop by hand. They hire a tractor for some of the farm work and use oxen for ploughing grooves in the soil to allow water to drain away. Harvested wheat

'Some men work on repairing the roads, or as labourers in the construction industry building houses.' – Mohammed Malik, village councillor.

Milking the family ▶ *buffalo at 5 am. Buffalo milk is used for drinking, and also to make ghee, which is a type of butter used for cooking.*

◀ A blacksmith making farm tools in Palak. Traditional trades are still in demand in the village.

is taken to the electric grinding machine in the village, to be ground into flour. Any flour that is not needed by the family is sold. Some farmers in the village own livestock, sometimes up to forty cows, which are mainly kept for milk. There are also chicken farms in the area.

About twenty people in the village own cars and five people own twelve-seater vans. They earn money by hiring them out for return trips to Islamabad airport to allow families to greet relatives visiting from abroad.

The local cobbler makes shoes ▶ for most people in the village. They are entirely handmade and are very hard-wearing.

Going to school

Education is very important to people in Pakistan. Many parents want their children to gain the qualifications that they never had the chance to obtain. Children may be sent long distances to go to a good school. Some wealthy parents even send their children abroad to go to school. Other families move to the cities so that their children can attend city schools, which have more money spent on them by the government than those in the countryside.

Government schools charge low fees, but they are more crowded and have less facilities than private schools. Many lack clean drinking water, a good electricity supply or even desks, so children have to sit on the floor.

SCHOOL IN PAKISTAN	
Times:	8.30 am–1.00 pm
Holidays:	June–August (three months)
	End of December (two weeks)

A student at a mosque school in Rawalpindi. Many children go to mosque school, where they learn to read the Qu'ran, after they finish ordinary school.

If they can afford to, parents send their children to the growing number of private schools in Pakistan, which have much better facilities than the government schools. Private schools teach either in Urdu or in English. Boys can also attend mosque schools, which give a religious education.

Children begin nursery school from the age of four. At about five years of age, they enter primary school. At nine or ten, girls and boys attend separate middle schools until they are fifteen, when they take an entrance exam to get into high school. At high school, pupils can take an arts or sciences course, or a course in industry and commerce. Some students then go on to take a university degree.

▲ *A school class learning outside at a boys' school near Skardu, in the remote, far north of Pakistan.*

Learning how to read ▶ *the Qur'an at a mosque school. The Qur'an is written in Arabic.*

School in Lahore

▲ *Resting between lessons at City College, Lahore. Although more boys go to college and university than girls in Pakistan, the number of girls continuing their education after school is increasing.*

Lahore has schools from nursery to university level, including many private schools. It is very difficult to gain a place at a private school because there is a lot of competition. Aitchison College is a famous private school in Lahore where Imran Khan, the cricketer, was a pupil. Government College is also well known, and trains students to go on to all kinds of professions, such as medicine and law.

Some people open schools in their own homes. Students from poorer families often teach younger children in order to earn money to pay for their own education. Many children are given extra tuition in their weakest subject, or in English.

◀ A chemistry practical lesson at the Punjab University in Lahore.

There are a number of ways to travel to school in Lahore. Umar Hussain is driven by his father, but his friend catches a scooter rickshaw. Other children catch a school van, or ride their bicycles.

Children in Pakistan have to work very hard at school because every year they have to pass an exam before going up to the next class. Sometimes children stay awake at night preparing for their exams.

▼ Extra lessons being given on the rooftop of a house in the old city of Lahore.

School in Palak

There are two government schools in Palak, one for girls and one for boys. Both take children up to fourteen years old, but the boys' school takes some pupils up to the university age of eighteen. The boys' school has much better facilities than the girls' school, and there are more teachers per student. The boys' school has eighteen teachers for 237 boys, whereas the girls school has only five teachers for 120 girls.

'When I finish school here I want to go to the school in Dudial. Then I want to go to college in Mirpur. I hope I can get into university after that.' – Wagida Akhtar, 8 years old.

▼ *A lesson at the girls' school in Palak, where a* dupatta *(headscarf) is part of the school uniform.*

Pupils who want to ▶ go to college in Mirpur have to catch this bus from the village.

Most schoolchildren in Palak get up at 6 am and walk to school, since both schools are in the centre of the village. The school day in both schools begins with assembly on the playground, after which classes begin. Many of the lessons take place outside because the school buildings can become crowded. The younger children write on a chalk board, whereas older children use pens and paper. Apart from the main subjects, which are taught all over Pakistan, students in Palak also study agriculture, which is only taught in rural schools.

▼ A maths lesson using chalk and a slate board.

At the boys' school, football and volleyball are played. The boys would like to play cricket, but a game of cricket takes too long to fit into the school day.

Sometimes pupils in Palak take time off school to help their families with harvesting or other farming activities. Some families are so poor that they cannot afford to pay for their children to go to school. Instead, these children have to work to bring in money for the family.

Pakistan at play

People in Pakistan work hard during the day so that they can enjoy their time off in the evenings. The weekend is on Friday and Saturday. Friday is the Muslim day of rest, when most offices, schools and businesses remain closed. Many people make weekend trips to bigger towns and cities. Popular activities are watching sports like cricket, relaxing in parks, or going shopping. On Fridays, all men attend mosques to pray for about an hour in the afternoon. Visiting a shrine or one of Pakistan's many historic sites or buildings is another popular Friday activity.

The coastal city of Karachi has the beaches of Clifton and Paradise Point, where there are camel rides and a funfair. People who live in the cities of

▼ *Traditional tea houses are still very popular in Pakistan. Tea is normally brewed with milk and sugar added.*

◀ *Camel rides on Clifton Beach, Karachi. The camel owner has made the camel sit down to allow people to climb into the seat on its back.*

FAVOURITE SPORTS IN PAKISTAN

Cricket	*Kabadi* (where two teams try to get into each other's territory)
Squash	
Field hockey	*Guli danda* (similar to hockey, with an elongated ball)
Volleyball	
Football	*Buz kushi* (similar to polo, played in the mountains)

Islamabad and Rawalpindi often head for the hills at the weekend, travelling to the cool, hill resort of Muree for a day trip. This is a beautiful place with many shops, including antique jewellery shops.

Many Muslim festivals are celebrated in Pakistan. In early spring, people dress in yellow and hold kite-flying competitions to celebrate the festival of Basant, the coming of spring. Other important festivals include Eid-ul-Fitr and Eid-ul-Azha, between February and April each year. Independence Day, on 14 August, celebrates the formation of Pakistan.

▼ *Video games are becoming more popular in Pakistan with young people who can afford them.*

Leisure time in Lahore

▼ *Cricket is played almost everywhere in Lahore, on the playgrounds, streets, car parks and even the rooftops.*

There are lots of places to go and things to do in Lahore, from picnicking in the beautiful parks, to watching cricket and hockey at the famous sports grounds. Evening shopping in the busy bazaars of Lahore is very popular. Lahore has many restaurants, ranging from pizza and burger bars, to those serving traditional Pakistani food, or expensive hotels like the Avari or the Pearl Continental. Some hotels have discos, which are popular with young, wealthy people.

An evening out at the cinema used to be a popular activity, but now most households have their own television and many have videos and satellite dishes.

'If I'm not playing street cricket with my friends, I like playing badminton at the sports centre.' – Shahnaz Afzal, 11 years old (left).

▲ *Modern shopping centres are popular with the young and wealthy in Lahore.*

Although there are fewer cinemas than there used to be, there is a big film industry in Lahore and most of the filming takes place in the city.

Millions visit the tomb of Data Sahib, the patron saint of Lahore, which is also a social centre. People go there to pray for whatever they wish, or to gossip, sleep or just relax. The tomb is usually covered with wreaths of roses.

When they are not watching television, children in Lahore enjoy playing sport and games such as street cricket, *guli danda*, hide-and-seek, marbles and ludo.

◀ *Playing a homemade game on a city pavement.*

Leisure time in Palak

At the end of a busy day in Palak, the men often get together to drink tea, chat and play cards. Women may meet up to watch a film or listen to music together.

▲ *A game of draughts in the early evening. Board and card games are very popular in Palak.*

Family ties are strong in the village and people often meet with relatives for dinner. Although there are no cinemas or restaurants in Palak, local entertainers, such as *qawwali* singers, sometimes perform in the village. Many young village men enjoy playing *kabadi*, which is a game where two teams try to get into each other's territory.

Weddings in the village are occasions for celebrating with food and dance. City wedding celebrations usually happen in the evenings, but in Palak, like other villages, they take place during the day and run over several weeks.

Villagers relax on a ▶ *charpois (traditional string bed) outside the tea restaurant in Palak.*

'Playing cricket on a dirt pitch slows the ball down, so you have to use all your strength to bowl. Perhaps that's why Pakistan has so many fast bowlers!' – Atif Khan, 13 years old.

▼ *There is much more space for playing cricket in Palak than in Lahore.*

There are sometimes parties thrown by local political leaders, usually in the time just before elections. On Independence Day, most people from Palak go to celebrate at the Mangla Fort, which overlooks the Mangla Dam.

Children in the village like flying kites and playing cricket. Rangzeb Iqbal and his friend often play cricket in the fields after harvest. When they do not have a cricket ball, they play with a tennis ball wrapped in insulating tape. Rules are strictly followed, but they usually favour the owner of the bat and ball!

The future

Pakistan is a very young country, which is growing fast. Since Pakistan was formed in 1947, industry, the amount of farm produce and the building of modern offices have all increased, and huge power dams have been constructed. However, there are large differences in the quality of life between rich and poor people, and women still have less freedom than men. The government is short of money and has trouble providing enough good education and healthcare.

As more people use household appliances and cars, and more farms use fertilisers and pesticides, pollution is increasing. Many cities are growing faster than their water and drainage systems can cope with.

The government is trying to increase the country's wealth by encouraging the growth of industry. There should be many more industries using modern technology in the future.

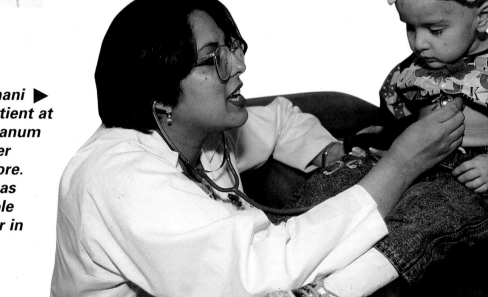

Dr Naheed Usmani ▶ and a young patient at the Shaukat Khanum Memorial Cancer Hospital in Lahore. As healthcare has improved, people are living longer in Pakistan.

◀ As in cities all over the world, beggars and homeless people are a common sight in Pakistan's cities.

The country has many natural resources of its own, such as oil, gas, hydroelectricity and cotton, which will be very valuable in the future. Instead of selling raw cotton abroad, more cotton is now being made into clothing in factories in Pakistan and then sold abroad. This creates more jobs and brings more money into the country.

Some of this money can be spent on education and healthcare, which should help to improve the average standard of living in Pakistan.

▼ Traffic is an increasing problem in many cities, as more people own cars and make more journeys every year.

IMPROVEMENTS IN EDUCATION

	Percentage of children going to primary school
1960:	25%
1992:	42%

(Sources: UNDP, UNICEF, UNESCO)

The future of Lahore

Lahore is a thriving city, where traditional cultures mix with modern life. But like many growing cities, parts of Lahore have problems of poor housing and overcrowding, traffic pollution, drainage and transport.

Overcrowding is made worse because the city is stopped from expanding to the west and north by the Ravi river, and to the east by the border with India. The government does not have enough money to provide more cheap housing in the south.

The government needs to spend more money on public services such as drainage and transport, especially in the old city, where traffic jams and air pollution are big problems.

Traffic is creating problems for the whole of Lahore.' – Imtiaz Abid, engineer.

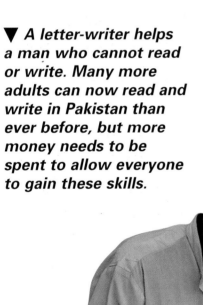

▼ *A letter-writer helps a man who cannot read or write. Many more adults can now read and write in Pakistan than ever before, but more money needs to be spent to allow everyone to gain these skills.*

▲ A traditional tonga competes with modern traffic for road space in central Lahore. Many city vehicles carry fare-paying passengers.

There have been many changes in Lahore. There are now organizations in the city that encourage women to train for professional jobs. Many women are now going into professions, from fashion and furniture design to medicine.

With its rich history and beautiful historic buildings, Lahore is the most visited city in Pakistan. Tourism could be a major source of wealth for the city in the future, which could be used to improve the lives of its residents.

◄ Abdul Wahid works on his PhD at Punjab University. Learning how to use modern technology is seen as a path to greater opportunities and wealth.

43

The future of Palak

Each year, the water-level of the Mangla reservoir rises as more silt is brought down by the rivers. In September 1996, the water lapped around houses near the edge of the reservoir. The water authority has warned owners of about twenty houses in Palak to move elsewhere to be safe. This problem is likely to get worse in the future and people may have to start building new homes higher up the hillsides.

Education has greatly improved in the village over the last thirty years. This has meant better opportunities for young people, many of whom will look for jobs in Pakistan's cities, or even abroad. However, it does mean that fewer people stay to farm family land in the village.

▼ **Silt from the rivers fills the Mangla reservoir, making the water-levels rise every year.**

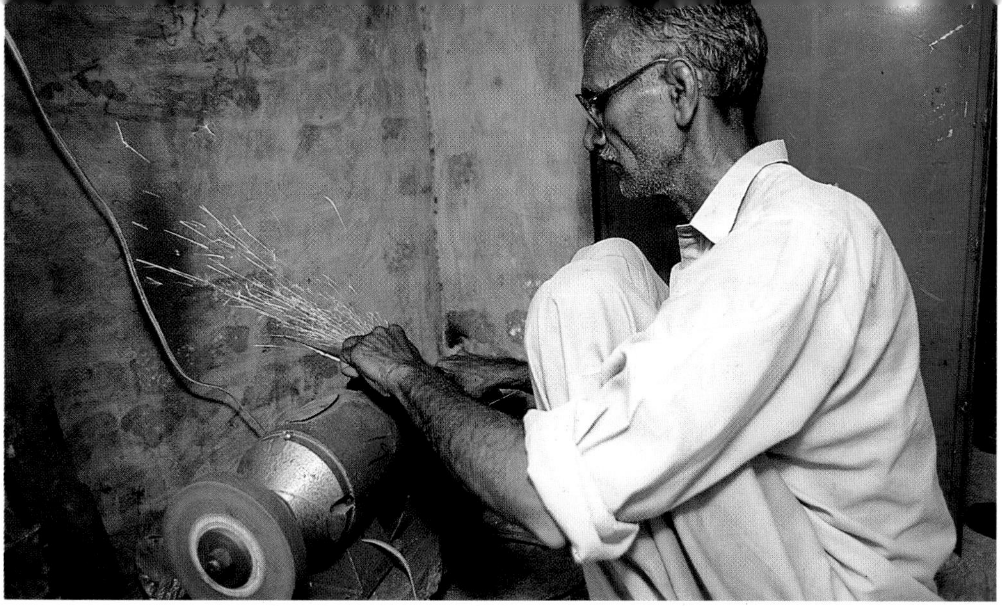

◀ *New technology is making manual work much easier for some villagers. This blacksmith is using an electric grinder to make farm tools.*

Despite these problems, life is becoming easier in Palak. There is enough money, much of it from overseas, to improve things in the way that people want. This includes improving the water supply, building roads to every house and improving the local medical clinic.

'Young people who leave the village to work in cities, or overseas, sometimes don't want to come back. But when they get older, they usually want to return here to their families. This is their country.' – Gulzar Amad, villager.

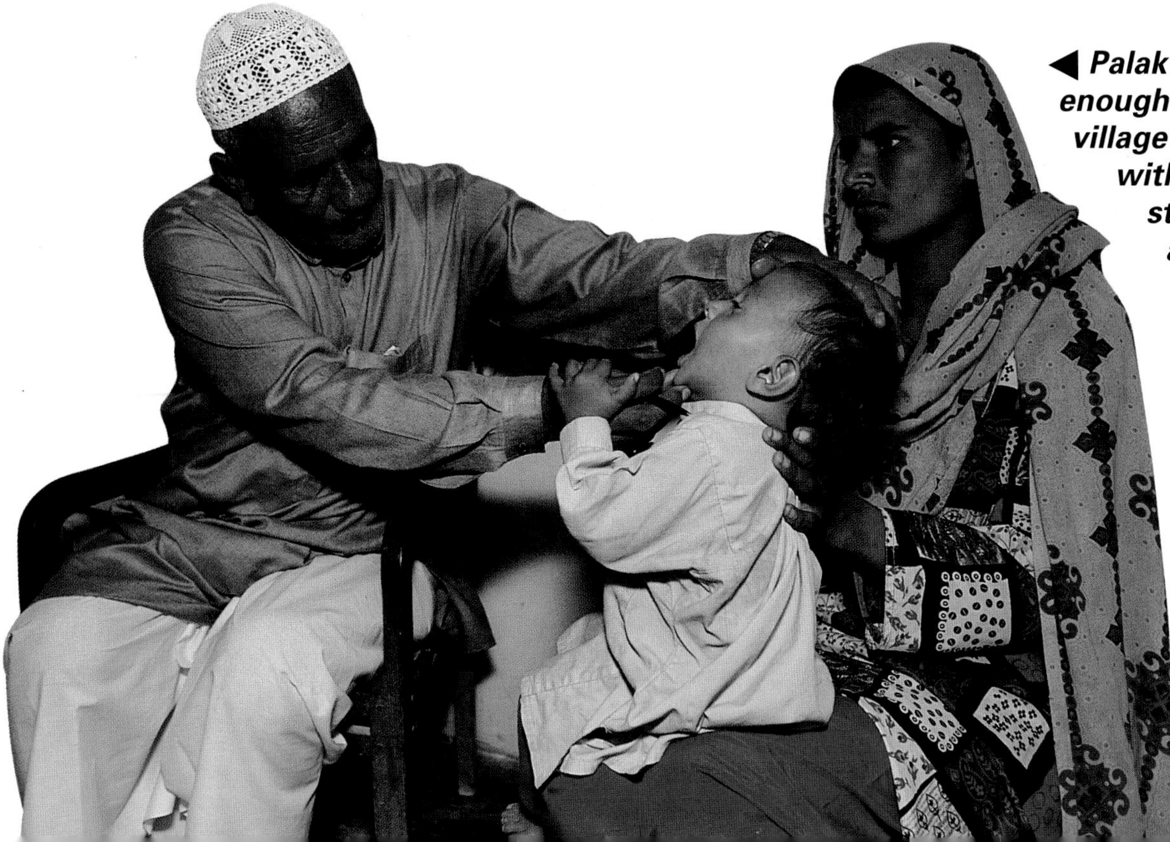

◀ *Palak is lucky enough to have a village health clinic, with five medical staff to look after villagers' health in the future.*

Glossary

Afghan refugees People from Afghanistan who have left their own country to escape the civil war that started there over twenty-eight years ago.

Air-conditioning A system of controlling the temperature in an enclosed space.

Bazaars A group of market stalls and shops.

Commemorates Celebrates and preserves the memory of an occasion.

Dam A strong wall built across a river to hold back the water.

Delta A flat, fan-shaped area of land where a river splits into many channels as it empties into the sea.

Dissolves Turns to liquid.

Disputed territory Land where more than one country claims ownership of it.

Floodgates Barriers on a dam that hold the water back.

Flood plains Areas on either side of a river where the river regularly floods and deposits silt.

Glaciers Rivers of ice that move very slowly down a mountain

Embankment An earth or stone bank for keeping back water, or for carrying a road or railway.

Evaporates Turns from solid or liquid to vapour.

Humid A climate with air that is warm and damp.

Imam A Muslim religious leader who leads the prayers in a mosque.

Irrigating Supplying land with water, using sprinklers, canals, pipes or ditches.

Lagoons Lakes separated from the sea by sandbanks.

Mangrove A type of tree that grows in muddy swamps, which has long roots hanging down from its branches.

Monsoon A strong seasonal wind of southern Asia. It brings rain in the summer months.

Mughal An Indian Muslim dynasty, which ruled from 1526–1858.

Provinces Territories or regions of a country, often governed independently.

Qawwali **singers** Singers of religious music.

Reservoir An artificial lake formed behind a dam, used for storing water.

Scooter rickshaw A small, two-wheeled hooded carriage powered by a person on a motor scooter.

Shalwar Kameezes South-Asian outfits, consisting of loose-fitting trousers and a long tunic.

Silty Filled with silt, which is very fine particles of mud and rock, carried by a river.

Terraced farming Farming on land that has been cut into level banks along the sides of slopes.

46

Further information

Books & packs

Continents: Asia by David Lambert (Wayland, 1997)

Daughter of the Wind by Suzanne Fischer Staples (Walker, 1991) A gripping story set in Pakistan's Cholistan desert, which follows a young girl's difficult journey into adolescence and finally an unwanted marriage.

Muslim Festival Tales by Kerena Marchant (Wayland, 2000)

Worldfocus: Pakistan by Elspeth Clayton (Heinemann, 1996)

PHOTOPACKS

Mangla: A study of change and development in Mirpur, Azad Kashmir and Pakistan by Eaniqa Khan and Rob Unwin (South Yorkshire DEC, 1995)

Gariyan: Transport in Pakistan by Maureen O'Flynn (Oxfam, 1992)

Pakistan: Change in the Swat Valley by Steve Brace (ActionAid, 1993)

CD-ROMS & OTHER RESOURCES

Change in Pakistan (posters) (ActionAid, 1993)

Mirpur and Azad Kashmir (Rotheram Metropolitan Borough Council Advisory Services Unit, 1996)

Useful addresses

ActionAid, Hamlyn House, Archway, London N19 5PG Tel: 0207 281 4101
Website: www.actionaid.org

Development Education Association (DEA), 29-31 Cowper Street, London EC2A 4AP will provide the addresses of local UK Development Education Resource Centres
Tel: 0207 490 8108
Website: www.dea.org.uk

Pakistan High Commission, 36 Lowndes Square, London SW1X 9JN
Tel: 0207 235 2044

Oxfam, 274 Banbury Road, Oxford \OX2 7DZ Tel: 01865 56777
Website: www.oxfam.org.uk

Unicef, 55–6 Lincoln's Inn Fields, London WC2A 3NB Tel: 0171 405 5592
Email: info@unicef.org.uk

World Bank
For statistics and information about individual countries.
Website: www.worldbank.org

WEBSITES
www.commonwealth.org.uk
www.geocities.com
www.newsunlimited.co.uk/pakistan
www.pakgov.pk/

Index

Page numbers in **bold** refer to photographs.